The Petaled Pages

Copyright © 2024

The Wheel Collective LLC

All rights reserved. No part of this book, in part or in whole, may be reproduced, transmitted, or utilized, in any form or by any means, electronic or mechanical, including photocopying, recording, or by any information storage and retrieval system, without permission in writing from the publisher (or the contributors and artists whose works are included in this edition), except for brief quotations embodied in critical articles and reviews.

Edited by Nicholas Kistler

Introduction by William Thomas

Cover Design by Lauren Bucklin

Instagram: @Lauren.e.felicity

The Petaled Pages

May, 2024

The Wheel Collective LLC

Boulder, Colorado 80301 U.S.A.

"Nature is only wild to those who separate themselves from her"

-Raven Grimassi-

Contributors

Mariella Story

@Mariella.Story

William Thomas

@river_mann_band

Audrey Houghton

@whatalovelyyday

Huck Shine

Darkleaf.org & @darkleafpublicatio

Nicholas Kistler

@beardyspiritualman

Johanna Hernandez

lyramagdalene@gmail.com

Jackson Kistler

Eric Fischman

Hannah Willis

Lauren Bucklin

@Lauren.e.felicity

Shannon Bucklin

Ryan Ellis

Lincoln Taggart

A Note from Your Editor

I am thrilled to help present to you the third edition of The Wheel Collective's quarterly periodical, *The Pivot no. 3: The Petal Pages*.

We've been doing this for about 9 months now, and each launch we have brings me fresh excitement and appreciation for the works of art that come across my desk.

With submissions from songwriters, teachers, poets, and a host of other interesting persons; I want to note, once again, the unseemly amount of enjoyment I take in reading everyone's pieces.

As per usual I am profoundly grateful to the core members of the Wheel Collective (William Thomas, Mariella Story, and Johanna Hernandez), without whom, none of this would be possible.

I would also like to extend my deepest thanks to everyone who contributed to this edition. I know that I am certainly excited that winter has turned back on its heels and warmer days lie ahead. It is my impression that the pieces submitted herein reflect a similar feeling as my own at this point in the season.

Lastly, I would like to thank you, the reader. Without your support independent groups like ours couldn't afford to do any of the fun and wacky artistic stuff we take such joy in doing. And if I may be so bold, it is my belief that the world would be the poorer for it.

So once more, on behalf of our artists, The Wheel, and weirdo creatives everywhere, thank you, thank you, thank you.

I hope you enjoy the following submissions as much as I have.

With peace,

-Nick Kistler

The Pivot: A Cross-Quarterly Collection

As the Wheel of the Year continues to turn, and Spring comes into full blossom, we are happy to present our third edition of The Pivot Crossquarterly. To briefly note, in this series of publications we are exploring the human place within the cycles of seasonality as demonstrated by the naturally occurring and timely creations of various artists, writers and other creatives from our community.

We believe that if we can cultivate an organic and truthful relationship with how our bodies, minds, spirits, and communities relate to the processes of the natural world, we can access something deep in our humanity. We believe that while cementing the value of the creative and their role in the society we are constantly taking part in creating.

For this edition of The Pivot, we are focusing on the cross quarter day—Beltane. Sometimes called Mayday, one of the Women's Days to the old Celts, and the fundamental fertility festival of the ancient world. This is when maidens dance tethers around the Maypole, the hyacinths return to the valleys, and the countryside is lit with blazing bonfires—all commemorating the development of Nature in all her glory into full and unabated Spring.

To me, one of the most beautiful things about this time of year is that any bashfulness displayed by the fledgling season, any hesitation shown by the sprout as yet unsure if that was truly the last snow, has been thrown to the wind. This is a time for joyful shouting from freshly planted gardens and for little kisses placed with care because every from might really be a prince.

As we come into the beauty of spring we are called as well to do cauldron work. If the maypole is the phallic symbol, expressing the masculine vigor and upward momentum of Spring; then the cauldron is the womb of the psychosomatic mission bell that is both our ground of prayer and our true north. We create the star we seek in the cauldron, garden the apple in the eye of our wild and beautiful divinity—we inspired and respired (and even conspired) by our own fruit-baring and feminine spirit. It is the union of these two expressions of fertility, the outer maypole and the inner cauldron, that create a proper ground for the full- force, and even fanatic, phantasm of the vernal vestige.

If it were not for this ecstatic display that we tie to spring with story, with songbirds and scattered clothes by a still frigid river; if it were not for Beltane, there would be no Summer climax, no Autumnal harvest. Just as if we had not had the initial impulse for the work of art in which we are all engaging, there would be no chance of us creating anything at all.

But luckily for us, the world continues to spin, the seasons dance their perfect dance on tens of thousands of feet, and we have artists like Lauren Bucklin sending us magical paintings to use as cover pages for these periodicals. A world of gratitude to all the creatives involved and a special shout out to Nick Kistler our Chief Editor and the only reason under heaven hat these periodicals exist.

With all the blessings we, The Wheel Collective, hope you enjoy.

May your petals spring forth!

-Will Thomas

The Petaled Pages

A Dedication

May all beings be in contact and connection with their personal fertility, may they find inspiration in the beauty of their own human nobility and when it comes time to choose one road or another may they choose the road less traveled.

May all beings find peaceful redemption in their own creativity.

May all beings be righteously angry, perfectly confident, and tastefully horny; and by the grace of the tiniest stigmata in the smaller wildflower may they smile because they have no other choice.

Gratitude to the world we are growing and grown from.

Gratitude to the Liver and the Living in each of us that keeps us on the road of untrodden life.

Gratitude to these bushwhacking souls and gratitude to the brambles, especially the brambles.

Gratitude to each of these creatives.

Gratitude to the human imagination,

the sun, moon, stars and the wonder they inspire.

Gratitude to our teachers in whatever time and form

for we would have little knowledge of this work

if they had not made the path and left it wild.

<u>An Invocation for The Midst of Spring</u>

In that we are one, we are many.

Cells and stars and organisms voluminous.

Armies and schools and constellations of the small,

growing us into something more than the sum of their parts.

The great mystery:

Though we are many, we are also one.

I pray we remember that both are true.

The Petaled Pages

The Wild Wings Fairy Tarot
By Mariella Story

Full Deck Available Late Summer 2024

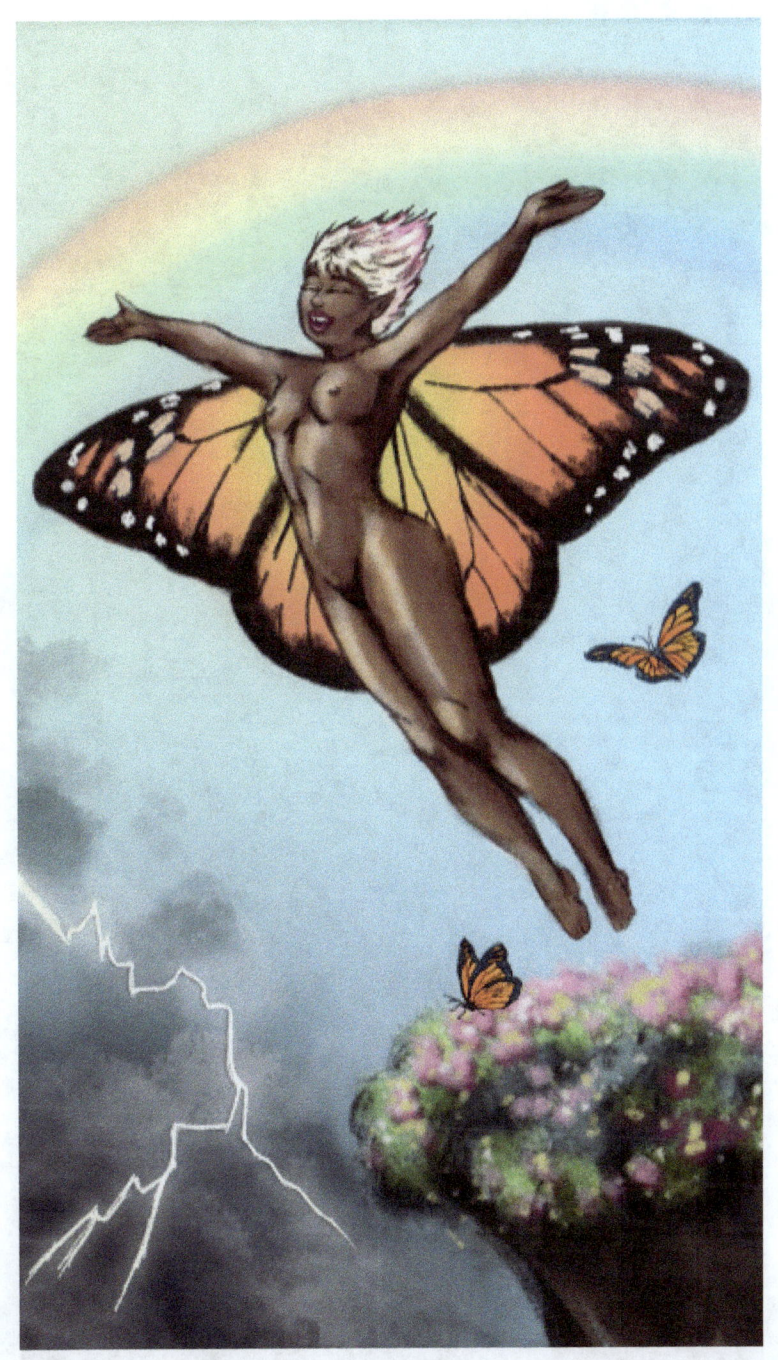

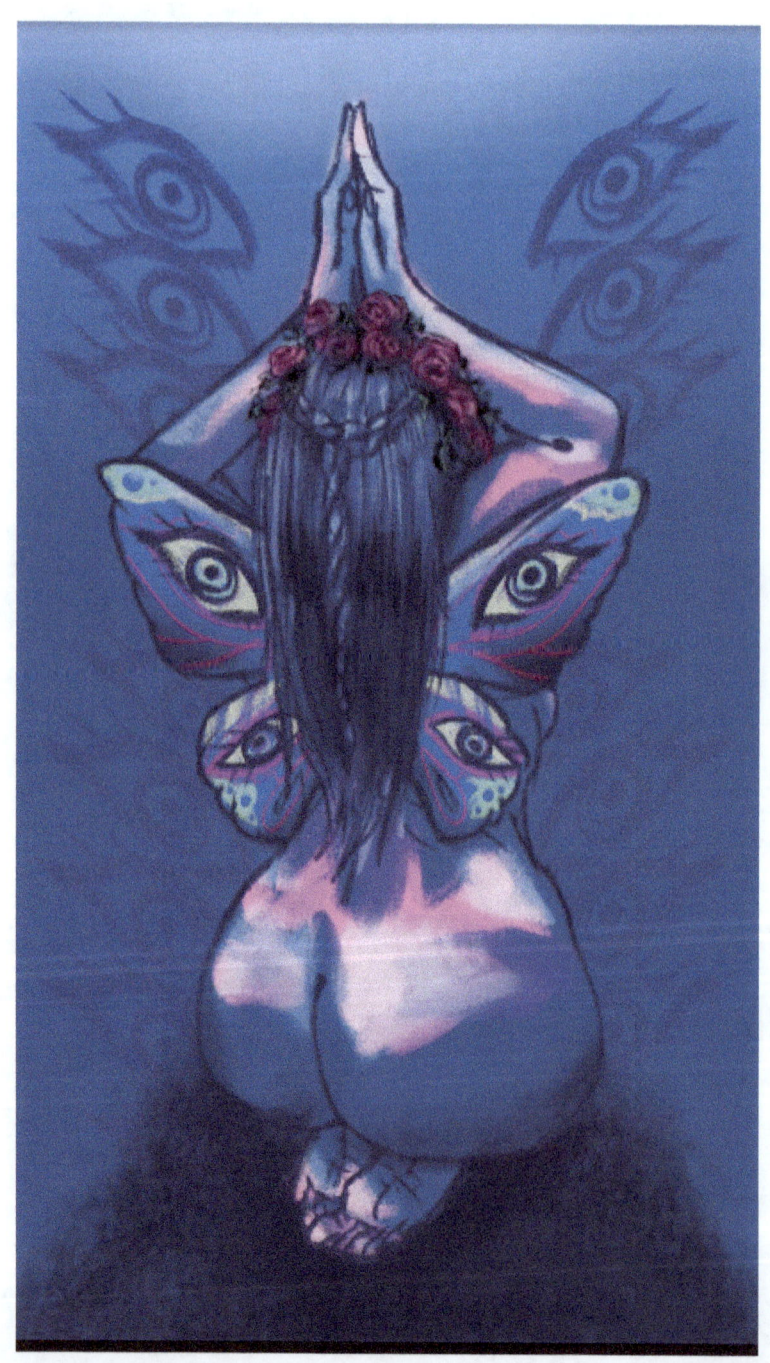

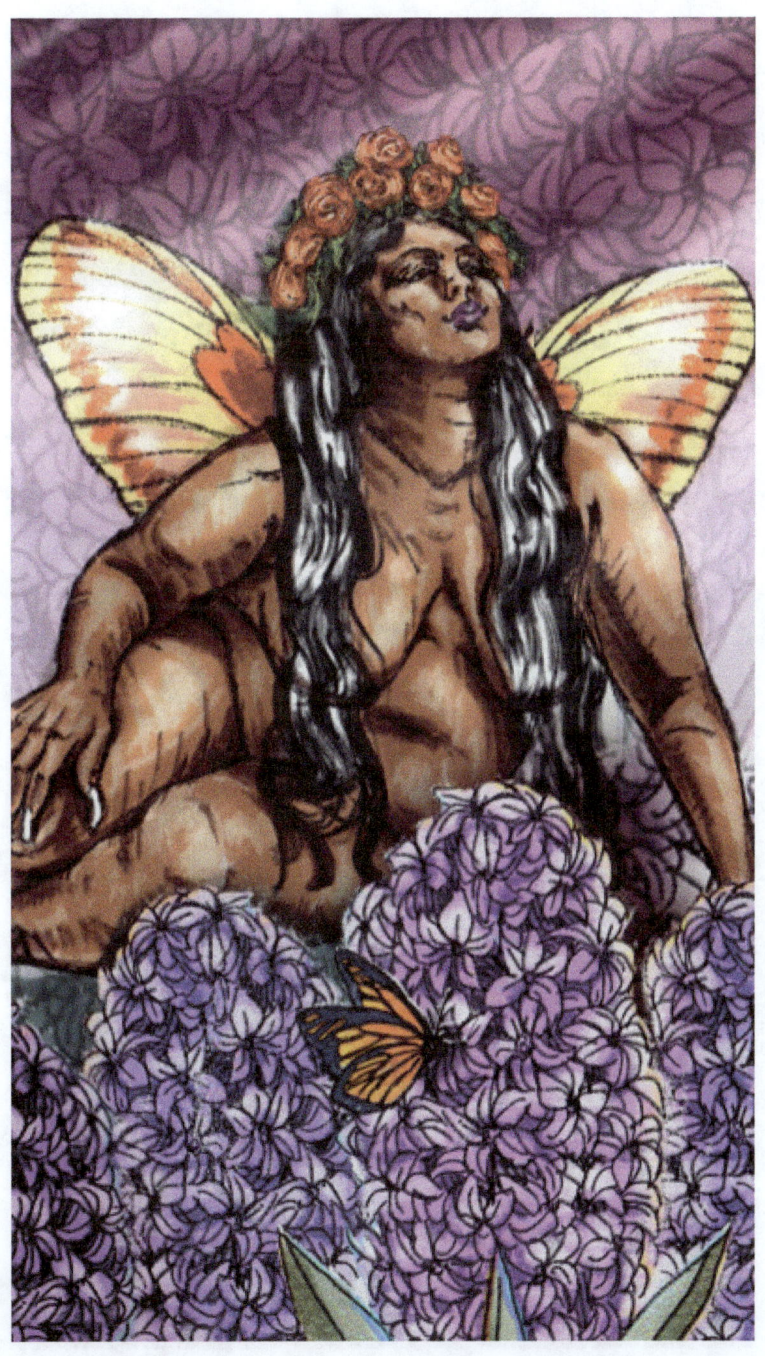

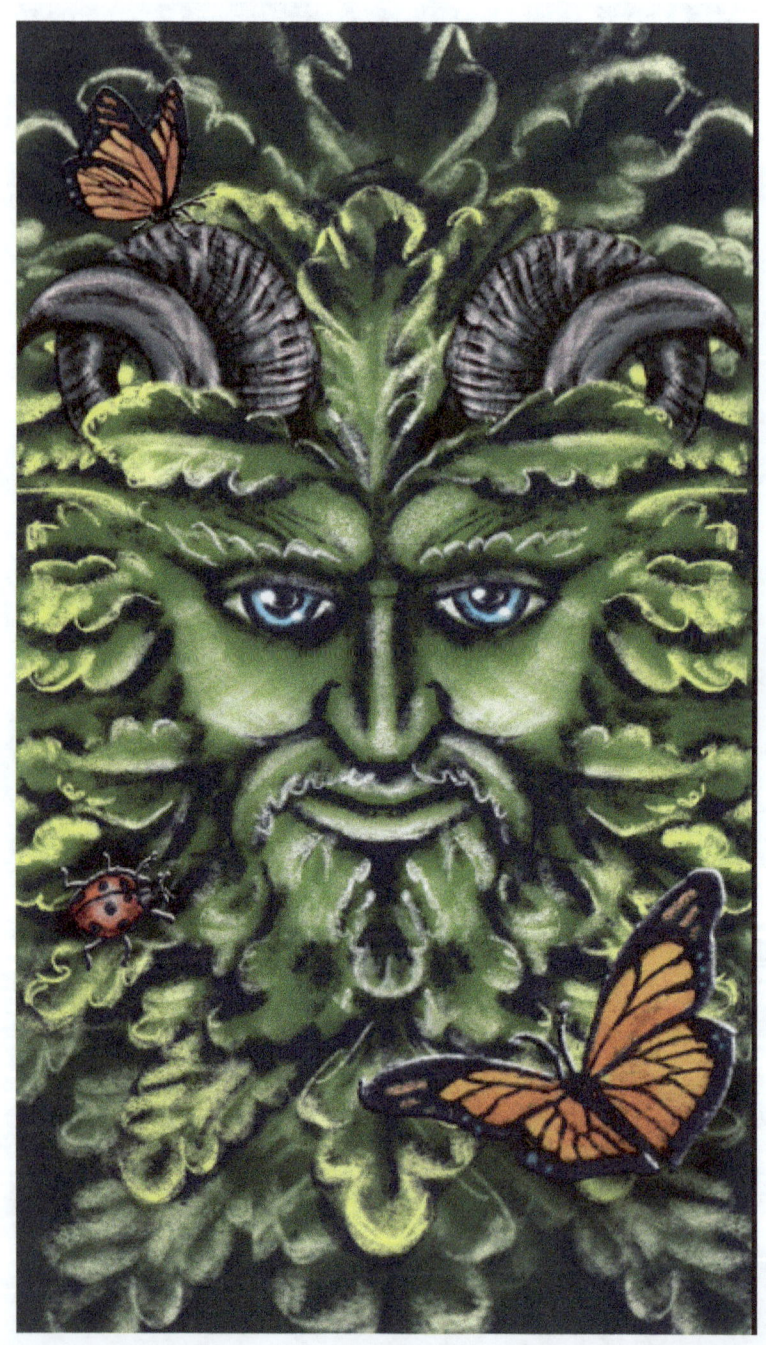

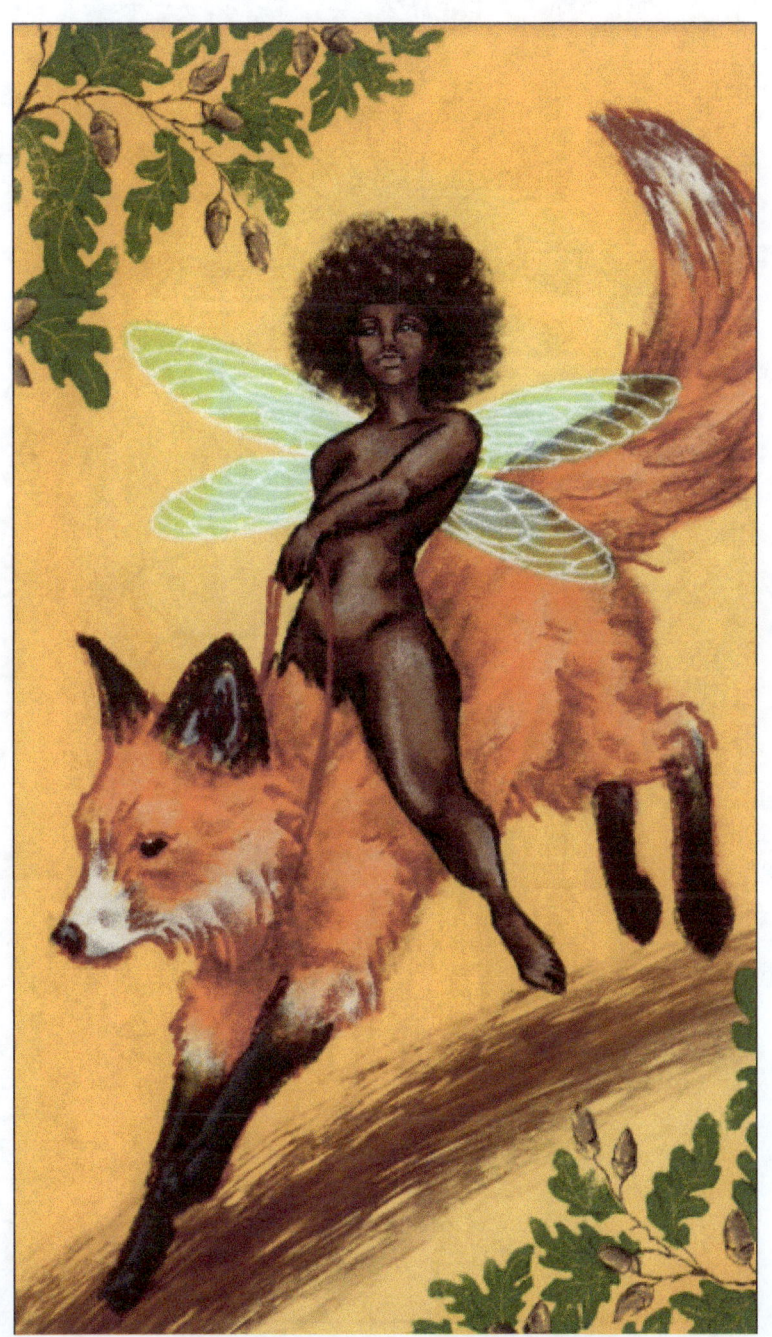

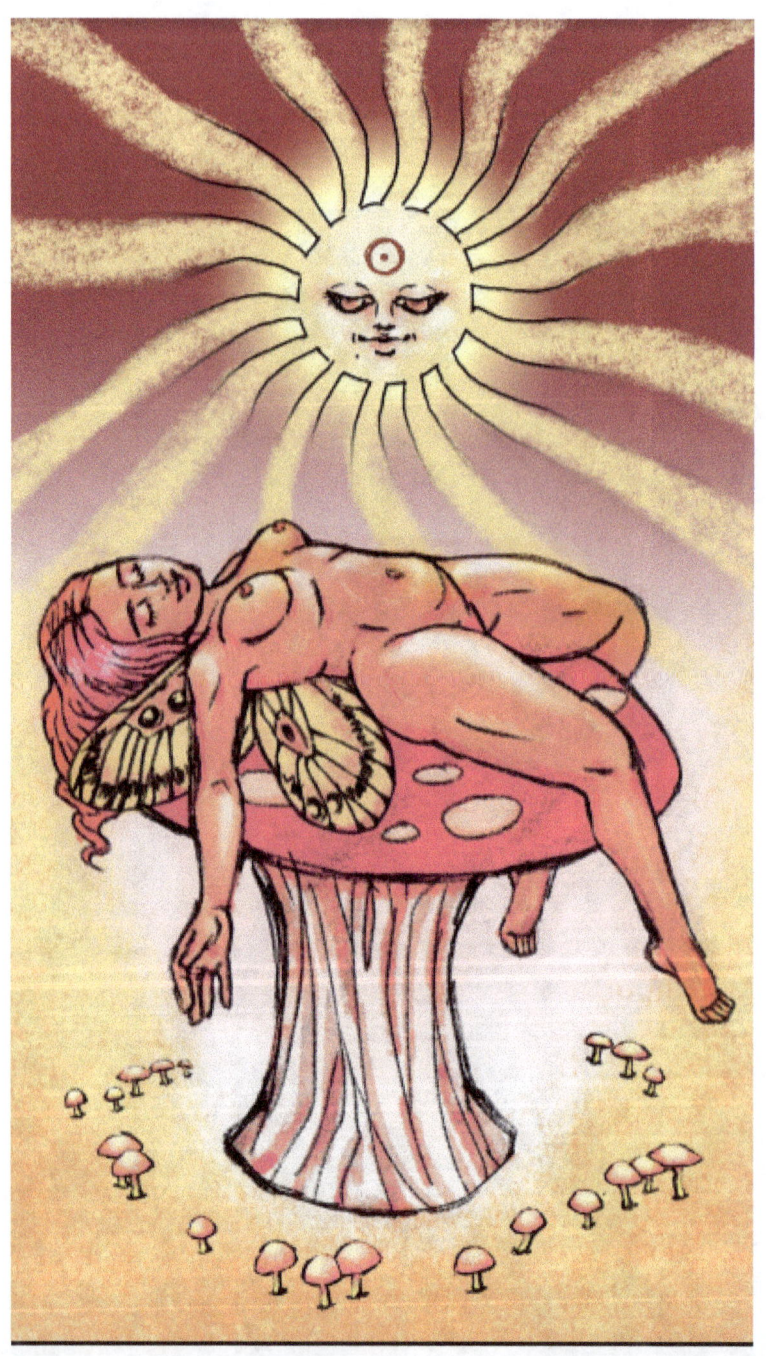

Selected Poems of Shannon Bucklin

-What the Trees Have Seen-
100 years still

100 years unmoved leaving no season to itself

A mystic dimension of courage to stay close to the way we were all made

Radical embodiment of what is released with each sigh

Turning inward once a cycle to move not faster than the speed of awareness

100 years still as a haven for despair carrying those who run and never want to be found in the same way again

No doors to close if don't want to be seen

No ears to plug if don't want to listen

Knowing resources only as a privilege and to be shared

Knowing the secret to life is that ants really like aphids and aphids really like umbels

A century sightless cleansed by the breath of winds, shaken by interior upheaval and rearranged by external temperament

Holding onto every version of self that's ever lived

Observe don't evaluate

Witness without analyze

100 years of recognizing loved ones solely by feel

100 years an identity to live in the midst of chaos, evading besiegement

An unthanked host of confluction

A misrepresented interpreter of an unspoken language

A limitless yet somehow overflowing container of treasure

A form often reformed under assumed permission

10 decades encouraging recovery from intensity

Having seen more than those in motion knowing richness estranged from monetary virtue

100 years having never been asked for a name or a story

100 years an undercover underrated over lover

100 years an under the covers plainly stated inner lover

100 years still

Sun sent

I came across an old journal entry the other day. On June 3rd 2017 I asked myself what does fullness feel like to you. Then left the rest of the page blank. I remember writing that, feeling empty and bare.
Special moments. Intimate engagements. Everlasting interactions.
A gift from the universe in the form of a shared moment. If time were to stop, I'd want to happen during one of those precious experiences.
Clouds take their turn making their presence known with a gentle thunderous hello. The sound guided you to the bridge to try and get a better listen. As you headed upstream I wanted to follow. As you journey I want to follow. I offered the self centered thought to a lead and watched it flow as it assured me the ease found in letting something go.
My mind followed my feet into the water. Ankle deep was enough to change my pace of breath. A familiar voice approached, curious about how the water felt. I was suddenly unsure of which entity was effecting my nervous system more; the creek or you?
With the clouds still shining, I began to undress and told you I was going in. Your eyes lit up signaling your eagerness to join. Each part of my body braced the ones above it as I waded deeper and deeper.
The moment we became still is one I will cherish forever. The clouds above us now shared the sky with the sun. The rushing water that filtered through us now glittered with light. We remained grounded by the rocks beneath our feet even though they have traveled further and for longer than we ever could.

I turned to admire the sun-sent glitter dancing on your skin when I noticed it wasn't dancing alone. Rain drops has effortlessly and harmoniously joined, following the sun ray's path one by one. I learned one time that there was a word for the greeting of rain meeting the earth.

What sets your Soul on Fire?
The free spirited wind flows through me as I journey. Loyal roots of plants remind me to be grounded and remain sturdy.

The sun illuminates my path, filling me with positive energy and light. The vastness of our planet keeps me humble and thankful for my sight.

Natural disasters and the human race teach me that resilience is KEY. Wildlife assures my desire to be free.

All four seasons promote opportunity alongside change. While natural weather can explain emotional range.

The flow of water inspires the motion of movement. Failure teaches room for improvement.

Our very own moon symbolizes divine power. The cycle of life lies right within the center of a flower.

Human-kind posses an innate desire for connection. While negative energy provides us with a lesson about infection.

My brain inspires me to indulge in complexity. My heart reminds me that pure love is a simplicity.

The nourishing energy from Mother Gaia assures the importance of touch. The stillness of each mountain teaches me there's no need to rush.

Those who came before us encourage the power of knowledge. What truly inspires you is important to acknowledge.

A wonderful evolution of personal connection begins at birth. Nature has inspired me to respect my time on this Earth.

Selected Poems of William R. M. Thomas

Lilac Valley And A Cave (What Cannot Be Held)

It is beautiful today, and i cling to it.
Cherry, rose, and some epiphany calling, Hail
Alondin! Spelling green with picture and breathing
I remake my heart daily, in the image
of a deity that is like snow.
I the dirty ground, angels
covering me in lilac valley
and a cave—where two people,
making love, remember Evermoore.
I challenge myself to Lorca,
bathe in the Hinayana
and cry for what cannot be held
while remaining clean.
I touch the wonderful things
with starlight that is my spit,
my piece of craving and infinity;
I kiss the ghosts that haunt me
and learning to dance
they teach the song of flowers
to the laughter between Heaven.
I made myself up
because the meadow
and the mirror
were taken from clay
on the second coming
of the first and final day.

What is it?

Let it through your body, as you stand there before your audience of only-breath; let it rain down on your own soft deity. Let it become you, and let yourself alone with it. Water roses and red begonias with it. Potentillas and paradise sing as you mumble it to a lover's breast, and the world cries out for it as you share your tears with elephants. Laugh long after, touch the sky with a high whistle and shake your fist at a concrete wall, it is there... behind you watching. Listening back to you like cassette tapes it rides in an automobile of human memory. It is the tonic of history, the reason melody makes sense, it cannot be uttered but it can be hummed. It cannot be held but can be loved.

(4/30/23) #1

Gather creatures
come to learn about the land
about the waves of timber
and koyote's laughter.
Place marbles on your eyes
and read what heaven wants from you
read it in the language
of blood and of begonias.
Bring your little destiny
tie it fast to the flank of saturday night
and ride on wind and weather
surrounded by beating hearts
that know what love is.

You hold the passing of ages
in your dancing feet.
Your cry of ecstasy
saves the world a little bit.
And you wake up sometimes
to find yourself glorious;
because you are simple flesh
and even simpler fire.
And your's is a fire
that cannot drown,
cannot dissipate
or surrender,
it kisses the water like kin
nestles in the ground
It turns blood into tribe
and makes Durga giggle.

Goddess Touch
the breath the sound
rises between us
and passing along the riverbed
out to that old crag
where harmony dwells
A human mouth
Sings Goddess Touch.

(4/30/23) #2

Dancing with you
was my perfect moment.
It was everything
and it contained everything.
I will chase that feeling
for the rest of my life.
Thank you my angel friend
for being true to yourself
for giving only
what was meant for God
and for awakening
(If only for a moment)
everything, everything
that makes me
so totally human.

Possibly Mayday 2023

You are first
and foremost
Woman.

5/2/23

I imagine that you taste
like bottled sunshine
the moon drinks
to make the night
animate and clean.
I picture your skin
like red rock
    let my fingers be the wind
and the space between us
be the water
that is implicit
in smiling.

In my mind
you wear nothing but vines,
In your hair
you keep dandelions
and between your breasts
hangs the fang if a fox
on a chord
of wrapped snakeskin.
I picture your eyes like the meadow
that will be the garden someday.
And your breath, to me,
is the answer to the question
that my body asked
when time began.

We gather our flocks
and tending each step
we walk down to the barrow downs.
We lay salt and tangerine skins
on a small rock between moss and agate.
We light a cigarette and never hit it
just letting it burn for the dead and fallen.

Then we take our swords and burry them.
Wrapped in silk and candle wax
they swoon for the ground's embrace.
Forgetting nothing we begin to burry each other.
We lie down and our bodies become
our own swords sprouting from the rape of love.

(5/3/23)

TWO SIDES OF THE SAME HAND
I want you to wear me
like dandelions in your hair.
Take me with you
into the shadows
when you go looking
for your body
in Avalon.
I have ten thousand hands
wrapped around you.
Special isnt it?
That we get to
love our idea
of someone.
Shatter me sideways
call everything into itself
and redeem the quiet.
Take your hands
lick the tip of your thumb
and put it in the candle flame.
Become a shade more tired,
smile at someone
and then crossover.
The land of Limen beacons you.
She calls you into her body,
lets you know she owns you.
Tempests crash against her breasts,
time passes through her veins,
and shadow is the smell of her hair.
She tastes like breath and vetiver
and rules the 8th day of every week.

A Visual Interlude
The Art of
Audrey Houghton

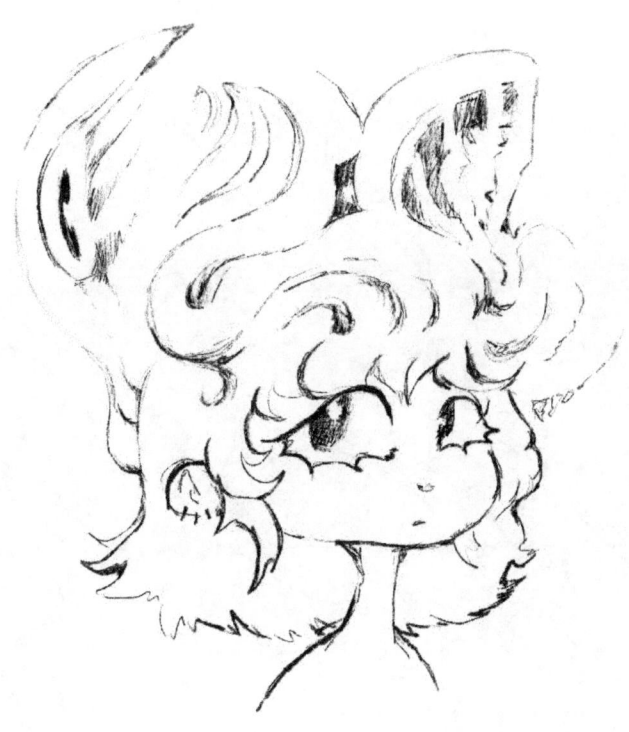

possesiveness

easier to deal
with when you
don't get attached

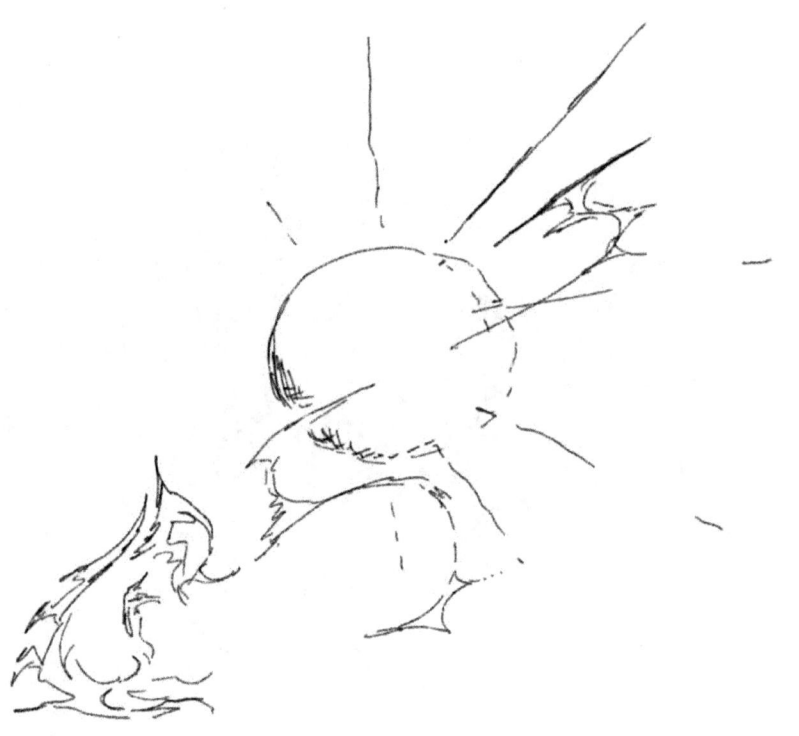

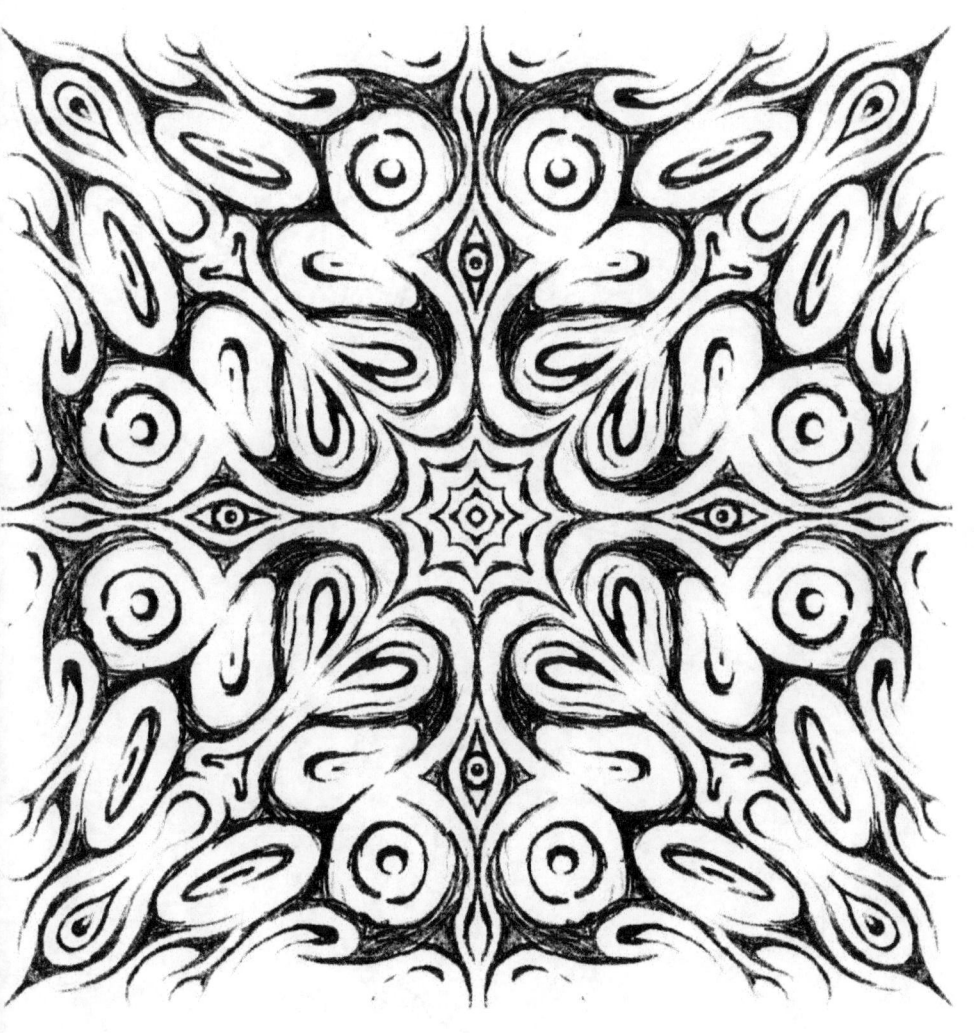

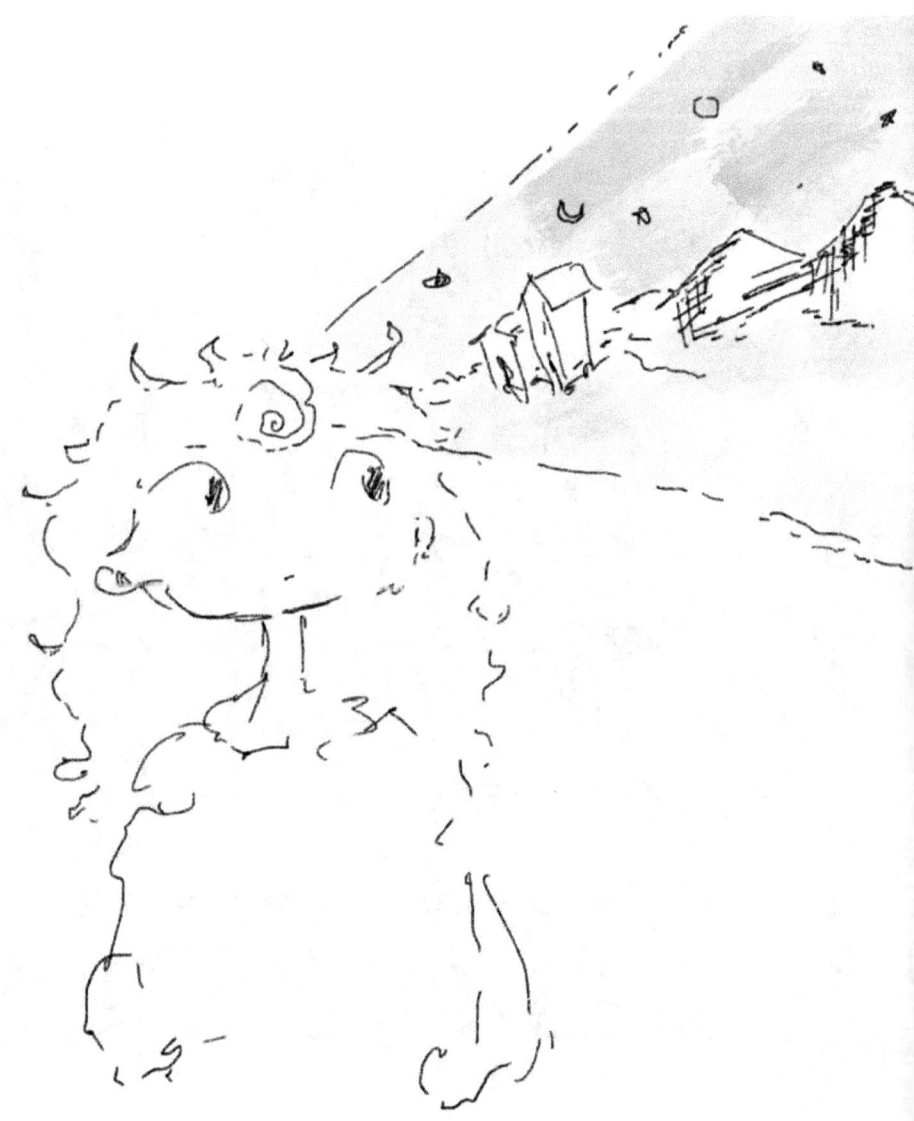

To Take a God
Grace Miller

To take a god, I washed with pine and whiskey.
I combed my hair down to my hips and dried it in the sun.
Water dripped off my breasts as I sat,
ready and willing, silent and still.
So it is with inflamed passion,
So with noble breath,
So with spirits high and lusty,
I enter the secret place of the gods.
They rub me in clover and raspberry.
Stoke, and kiss, and kindle.
It is in the highest points, that we pray.
I am laid on the Altar.
left there, all stretched and open.
Hours passed until there was no time.
The moon halted in the sky.
Comets rained into the glen.
My ankles drip with honey.
He comes across the fields and kneels before me.
All eyes and heart and chest. We stare, then strike.
His kisses are like firelight.
I open my mouth as I am entered.
High cries, and pink mounds.
Undulating currents, we thrash.
Heart stops, and I cease to exist.
Yet I call upon Thee.
OH Emptier of Oceans and Creator of Distance
The Full guiding Star in the boundless swirling
Spirit beyond the gods.
In shuddering shatters, I break free of all bondage
MY joy spills through the Universe,

Leaking into every crack, the Speaking Unspeakable,

for I am the wind beyond the SEA.

When I open my eyes, I see not the god, but a man.
Human breathing, and looking at me.
We smile and turn into each other.
Knowing the truth in Earth,
The alchemy in the form,
For we have become the Love that governs all.

Selected Poems of Johanna Hernandez

The call of the Space between the kiss is equal to the touch of lips
Gaps between the ecstasy laze at the altar.
In their disquieting hips, they carry the truth ecstasy forgot.

Nothing is constant. This is constant.

The shining bubble of personal wallowing is punctured by Love.

Here is going to lead me to terrible places, but terrible places have led me here.

Does God ever get lonely?
So many people.
Always asking!
So few people listen.

Johanna's Recipe for Red Pepper Pasta Sauce

-Roasted Red Pepper Pasta-

Ingredients:

3 Red Bell Peppers
1/2 Onion
4 cloves chopped garlic
Salt and Pepper to taste
4 Tablespoons Nutritional Yeast
1 Can Coconut Milk
Pasta, any kind, but fettuccine is nice.
Optional: red chili flakes, parmesan

Instructions:

Place bell peppers in the oven on broil. Watch until the skins are roasted.

Take the pepper out
and cool.

Chop them and fry them in a pan with olive oil, garlic and onions until the onions are caramelized.

Add them to a blender, with coconut milk, black pepper, salt, and yeast.

Blend.

Apply to Pasta.

Eat.

The Selected Poetry of Huck Shine

Into the Oracular Through a Woman Shaped Window
(An offering to Maria Sabina)

The scholars   went

The wise ones   went

The ones that knew the answers   went

The doctors and the scientists   went

They went and they left you alone

With the poets   went

With the revolutionaries   went

With the forgotten ones…

What authority do you choose to recognize little one

and when will you begin to heal yourself again

A Spring Poem

Springtime skies

have set upon me again

Violently

With such an assault

of green

of floral scent

To this my grief

did not consent

Watching Mother Fall

Watching Mother Fight

And so,

here we go again

at the end of all good things

Her twisted craft

and her spinning secrets screaming

were never going to be enough

not against what has come

Now full becomes the crucible

      comes the void

And so she flies

from the lake into the loon

down the mountain into June

a river of cold moonlight

Comes her wrath

Comes her might

What I Give to the Child Healing Inside

Take from me these desiccated flowers onceling

Try to remember they were harvested

in the sun of the solstice

and that they died and dried

inverted on witch's swing

Blood to the head, a playing child asmile

which death has left somehow in a shimmering moment

though   a truth is

When thinking of time one could say

all was a willing sacrifice

> but why must life be taken in order to live
>
> cries the child
>
> I wish to soak my life force from our Sol star
>
> cries the child

So I burn – I burn this body as offering

I send this smoke asky as penance

I set fire to these flowers as apotropea

I will burn my one life to ash.

As Living. As loving.

Yes   Make a joyful noise!

I will burn bright as a ray of light and color

May the Godmind suck up the smoke of me

and in all of their androgynous grandeur

sing a sweet sad song of full sails

and of grief upon the wind

May they then blow my soul tumbling backward

into whatever next is coming

A Dance Performance
by Ryan Ellis

A Visual Interlude

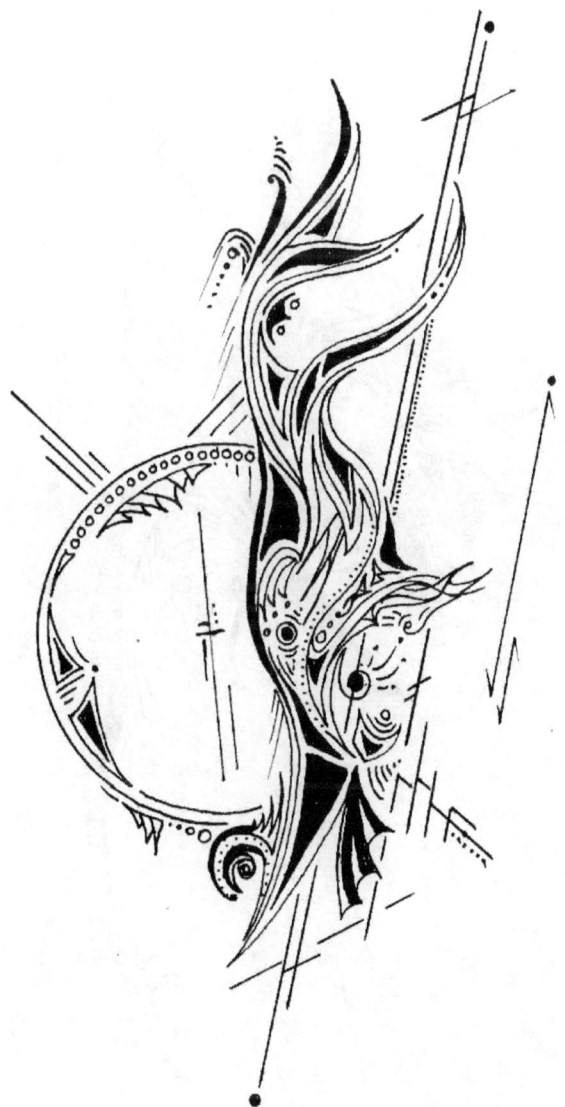

The Art of Jackson Kistler

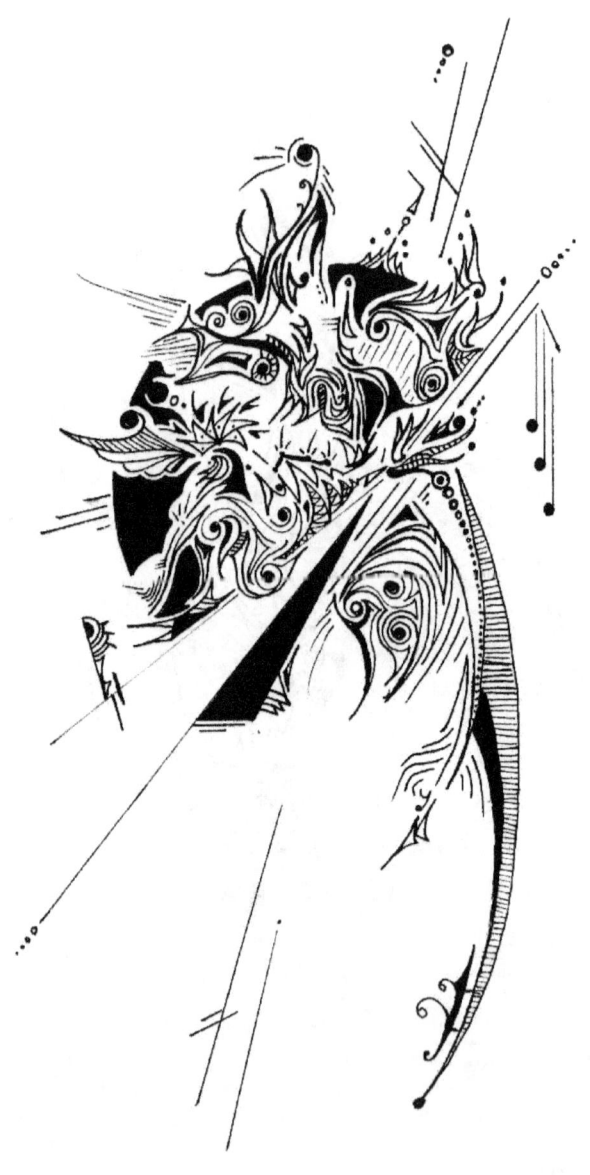

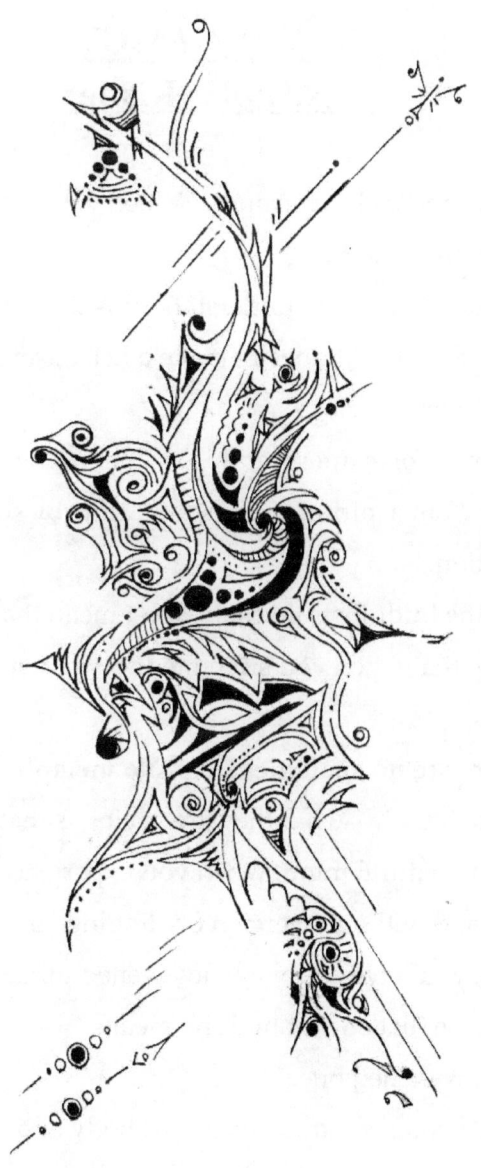

Notes From an American Meditator
Nicholas Kistler

A teacher said to me once, "When you sit in meditation you are the Buddha."

It took me years to understand this teaching, because as profound as it is, it doesn't make a lick of sense to the novice practitioner.

A ton of folks interpret this as "I'm doing what Buddha did," or "I'm aspiring to be like Buddha by sitting in meditation."

But the Buddhists teachers don't mean that. They mean, literally, that when you sit in meditation, you *ARE* the Buddha.

There are no analogies here. No metaphors.

Quite literally, what they are saying is that when you drop into natural mind, when you experience the world clearly and without aversion or clinging, just being with what is, you have cultivated awakened mind.

Because that's what buddha means.

The awakened one.

When you drop into awakened body and experience your sensations without clinging or aversion, just being with what is, you have buddha body.

When you sit in meditation, you don't just aspire to embody the energy of the awakened one; you embody it there and then.

This is your birthright, your natural state of non-judgmental awareness.

It's much like the transubstantiation of the Catholic mass, whereby the communion wafers and non-alcoholic wine *literally* become the body and blood of Christ. But instead of fusing our body with the body of Christ, meditation plugs us into our true natures as beings in the present voluminous moment. Which, if you're a feeling a bit on the wild side may well be the same thing.

Your Buddha Nature Is Right Here

This experience is what every Buddhist teacher I have ever studied under refers to as our buddha nature.

Our awakened nature.

Because buddha literally means "The Awakened One."

If we experience our true nature, we have the nature of the awakened one.

If we experience our natural body, we experience the body of the awakened one.

If we experience natural heart, we experience the heart of the awakened one.

Enlightenment, as coveted as it is, has always been only a breath away.

Nothing Special

One of my more unhinged teachers (and one who I am in great debt to) called this awareness the awareness of nothing special.

He referred to the process of awakening as the process of disenchantment. Of seeing that the game of enlightenment and spiritual progress and magic and all that is just a total load of horse shit.

And once we realize that, once we realize that the spiritual pipe dreams we've been fed, of special powers, and titles, and status all fall away, *that's* when we get a shot at true freedom.

Don't get me wrong. I'm down for the powers and intuition and magick. All that stuff is great. But true freedom is really nothing special. It's been in front of us the whole time, but our minds have been too clouded and hazy to notice.

The practice of meditation is all about just allowing our minds to settle. Like clouded water that naturally clears when left undisturbed, so too will our minds become clear when left undisturbed.

The Best Way to Allow Our Minds to Settle is Meditation

Most people are bad at meditation.

I can feel some of my teachers cringe as I say that, but it's true.

Most people can't concentrate worth a damn. They can't focus on the breath. They're busy thinking about lunch, or their ex, or their asshole boss, or some damned foolish thing in the Balkans.

And this is because most people treat meditation like an activity they have to master. Like a challenge they have to overcome.

It normally goes like this.

They sit down and "focus on the breath," because for whatever reason that's the single instruction from the anapanasati sutra that made its way into popular discourse for beginner meditators, (even though that sutra was *only* given to the buddha's disciples after they had already been practicing for quite some time.)

And invariably, most folks can't manage it.

Because, if we're being honest, focusing on the breath is <u>boring.</u>

Even for experienced meditators, counting inhalations and exhalations can be like watching paint dry.

(That's why this instruction was only given to monks who had already attained some degree of concentration. It's a route to something called Jhana; a state of deep blissful trance which beginner meditators are not expected to approach for quite some time.)

Not to mention the fact that most folks would literally rather do just about anything else than be alone with their breath, not to mention their thoughts.

I read one study where something like 67% of American men would prefer to literally electrocute themselves than just sit alone with their own thoughts for a mere 15 minutes.

Thankfully, the point of meditation isn't to "focus on the breath." Or repeat mantras, or silence the mind, or gain magic powers of focus and cure your depression and bust your anxiety while scoring the hot yoga babe at your gym.

I mean, you can do all that stuff if you want, but those are just the techniques. And as a teacher of mine is fond of saying, "The technique is not the practice. The practice is how you engage with the technique."

The *practice* of meditation, no matter the technique, is to rest your weary mind and body.

The practice of meditation is to come home to the present moment. Again and again, as much as you have to.

Because so much of our suffering stems from ignoring what's right in front of us, the cure is being with what is.

You don't have to focus on the breath to be in the present.

The breath is only one part of the present anyway.

As I said, most beginners start with what's called an object of meditation, (the breath, a sound, the rise and fall of the chest, etc.) because some folks decided that it might be easier to pay attention to just one thing rather than everything at once.

I personally started with something called a mantra (and I'd recommend most folks do the same) but once you develop concentration, you can widen your support structure.

By expanding awareness into sound, sensation, breath and just presence writ large, practitioners encounter what some Buddhists call "The Great Perfection." I've heard it called the diamond, I've heard it called is-ness, but the easiest way to conceptualize it is as the here and now, complete and effulgent.

No technique required. No real effort required. Just being with what is, is enough.

Selected Works of Hannah Willis

Desert Wind

I sat, half-naked, in the dry and exuding sun of the Great Basin Desert and listened to the chuckling Pinyon Jays. There were two at first and then a couple dozen within the hour. Their blue-gray wings tossed playfully in the undercurrent of a great sandy wind. They dipped in and out of the Juniper trees and cried out particularly loud when roosting on the Pinyon Pines, perhaps in excited awareness of the Pine Nuts that I had so greedily snacked on minutes before. The clouds turned crimson on the horizon and through the dewy atmosphere I could hear a whisper which I later understood to be the uncertain churning of the wind. The whisper grew and grew, until even my thoughts were no match for the bellowing.

It has been recognized widely amongst poets, musicians, and Pinyon Jays that the wind bears with it a deep and lonesome wisdom. This wisdom is granted to those who are open enough to receive it, but it's been warned that upon ingestion of such wisdom one can start to notice side-effects. These side-effects vary in substance and severity with the least worrisome being messy hair and the most intense being wandering feet.

This phenomenon is most true when speaking of the desert wind. I had felt it all summer after my first encounter on Comb Ridge in the Bears Ears Area, in fact, that itch in the soles of my feet. I can't boast that I gained all or nearly part of the wisdom that the wind plead for me to digest that night, but I think I now have an inkling of something. A distant remembering. Maybe even less than that. Our conversation now feels more like a dream than anything, but I do know it was real. As real as the streaked-throats, pale blue coloration, and dark-eyes of the Pinyon Jays. As real as the sandy grains that dug themselves under my eyelids in conjunction with those god-forsaken biting gnats. As real as an apparition of some mythical beast on the horizon of the airy and silver skyline.

    There she is now. Calling, pleading, pulling. Begging for me to step out of my comfort zone and follow her. She guides me with the tiniest hits of intuition, with a feeling of love that wells up from my chest, and the dancing grains of the red desert sand.

A Bike ride to the Sea.

I woke up on the 16th of June to a call,

well two actually.

The first was a call from my mother-

telling me of the passing of a dear friend.

The second was a faint whisper-

a calm, deep knowing inside of me.

It reminded me that somewhere-not too far away

the liquid heart of the universe was beating,

On its inhale, mudflats revealed shorebird feeding grounds,

the exhale a comforting wash of silver sea over tired toes.

So, I grabbed my bike and rode to the shoreline,

Certain that my grief would be best understood

In the lonely fashion.

I threw myself in and allowed the waves to thrash my body over the rocks.

I was sure that in some book somewhere this moment defined true paradise.

Even still- the freezing, salty water threatened to drown my lungs.

In a panic I asked, "what is it I should do?"

But the ocean deposited me sweetly on the shore and said nothing,

Apparently with better things to do.

So, I rode and rode,

The rusty old skoolie bike up the road,

And remembered the first time I met the ocean as a space explorer in grade school.

She had told me then, to listen, to pay attention.

That only in the cessation of my activity would I be satisfied.

I glanced back towards her, once, before pedaling on.

Feeling foolish that I had forgotten.

Artificial

My weight shifts under polyester sheets,
Micro-chemicals seep their way into my bloodstream,
Straight into the dream-state.
Perhaps more awake now than in the waking hours
When nerds behind white fiberboard desks, the global industrial workbench,
Decide what I will do what my time.

My eyes struggle back and forth under closed eyelids
Like colonies of ants searching for crumbs on the heat-soaked pavement.
I wonder what it would have been like to sleep at night when the trees wove the sheets themselves.
Asleep on the cold dirt floor, beneath yucca branch and falling spiders.
When I go to sleep under the Juniper tree, she feeds me.

When I go to sleep within the confines of the four-walls meant to protect me,
I am happily contradicting the great dirt mother of death and decay.
The white-popcorn walls fill me with ease,
And with benzene, chlorinated solvents, xylenes, cadmium, chromium, inorganic lead, styrene, and aromatic dyes.

When I wake up, I have an urge to sleep longer,
Let the great mother of synthetics lull me under her sweet embrace.

I powder my face with Paraformaldehyde, methylene
glycol, and mercury because the beauty industry tells me
that I won't feel so damn alone if I
don't look like myself.
I can feel the Isopropyl parabens from my cosmetics
disrupt my hormones and harm my reproductive tract. I
can feel my very DNA mutate and
change.

Good, let it be that way.
Smile through the pain.
And let flocks of Gulls fight over who will get the leftover
big mac.
Let them choke on the remains of my hunger to belong.
Let them crash into the sea.
Let them decompose into microplastics.

There was a time I would have sat along the shoreline and
watched the seabirds.
But now the only peace comes in numbing.
They are already dying anyways. So fuck em.
Fuck the birds and the insects and clean air and fuck the
plants that have the power to nurture.
If it's all burning down anyway, let me burn right with it.

Give me that sweet dopamine rush instead.
One more like. One more follow. One more package from
amazon. One more vegan leather handbag.
Tear out the oak and cedar and replace it with Bamboo.
Clear cut the old growth Eucalypt Forest of South
Australia and replant it with a monoculture of pines.

Sustainability is hot after all.
Get me high on pharmaceuticals.
Indoctrinate me with me fear.
Manipulate my thoughts with targeted ads and algorithms
And then kiss me goodnight with Fluoride and artificial sweeteners.

A Visual Interlude
The Art of Lauren Bucklin

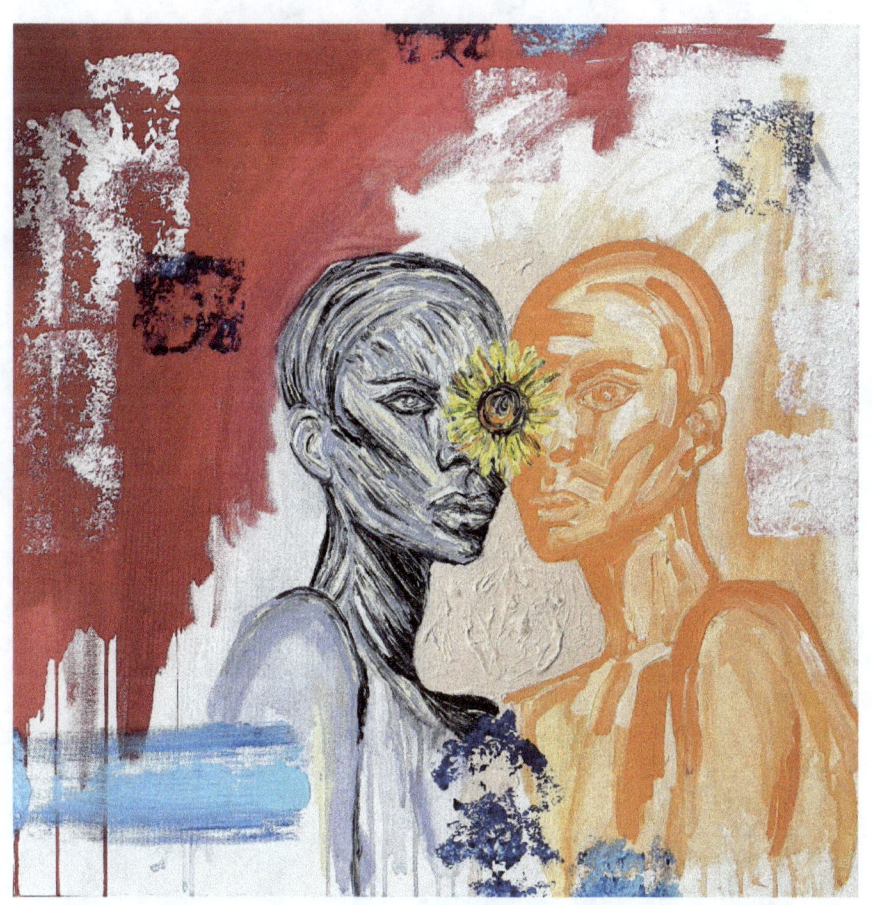

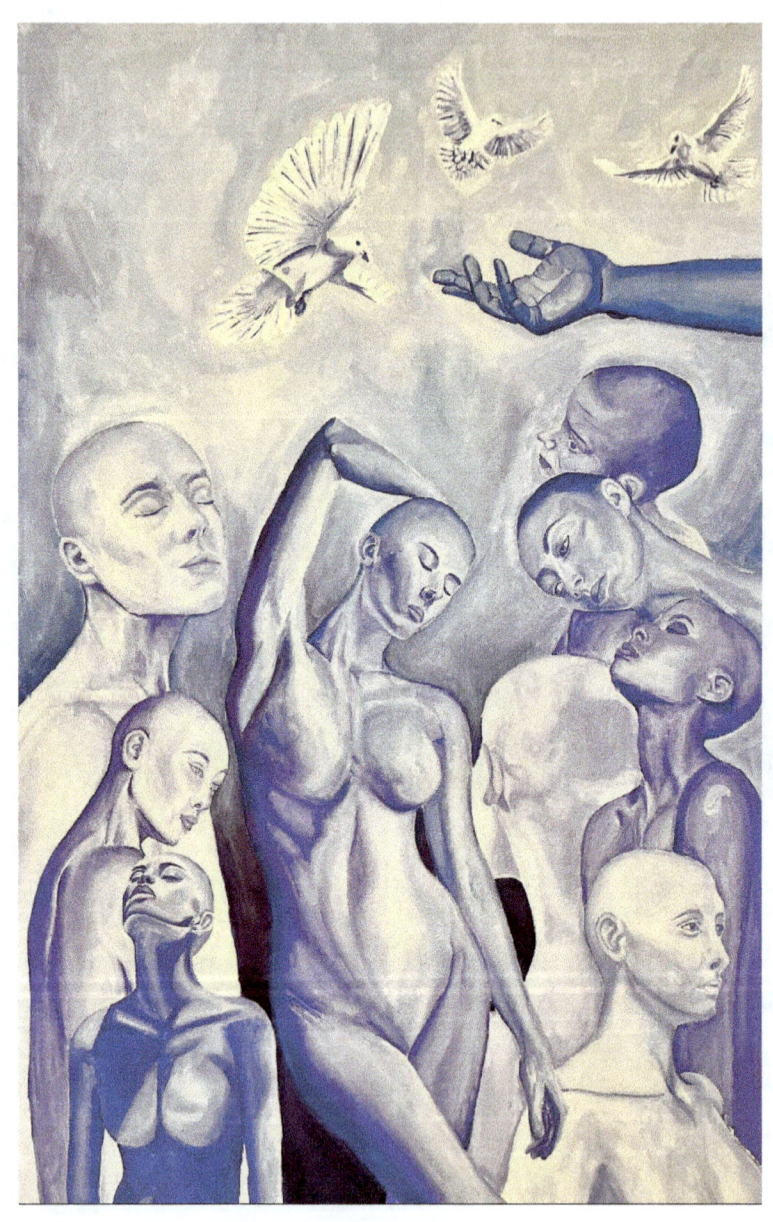

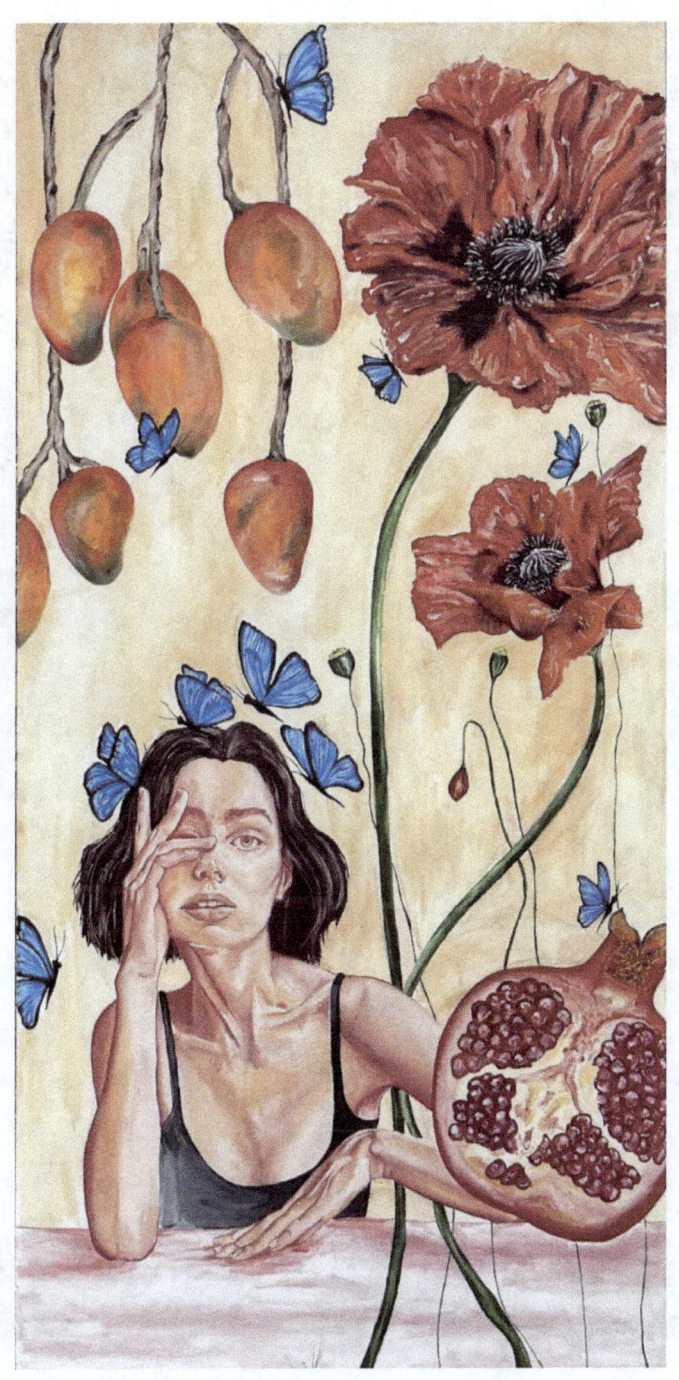

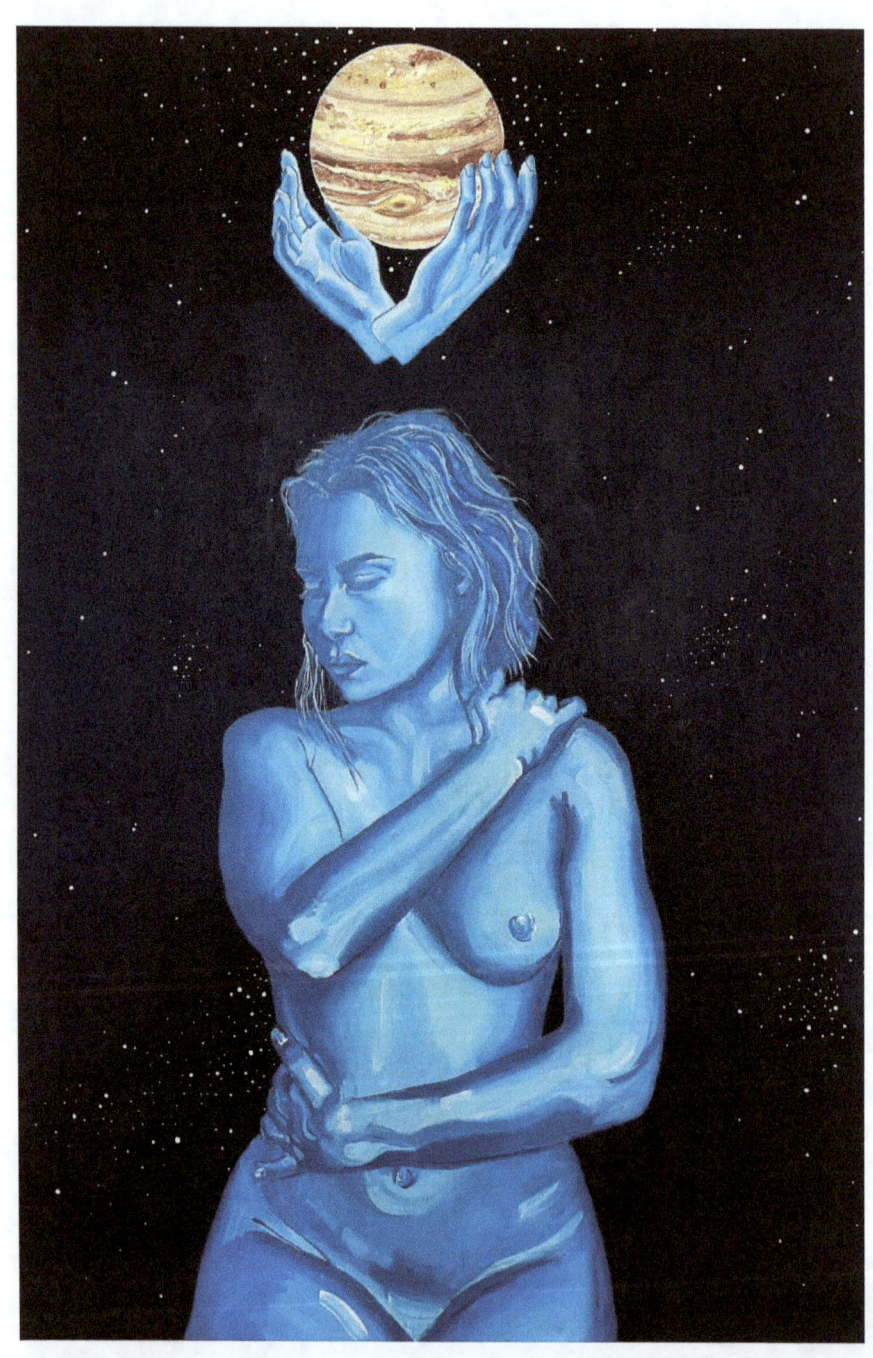

Selected Poems of Lincoln Taggart

Chain Linked Reality(?)

My dad's face turned into Mississippi.
For a moment someone gave him a permission
Slip
To take off his outfit and reveal a true face.
Not a name and location
But unforgotten tendrils of a
Past
Chained to the back of his forehead,
Embedded in links on links of
Memory
Defining a certain shade of hallucination.
Seeing is like a bolt cutter.
So when he shows his face,
Don't look away
(for all beings)

Woo-hoo!

I lost my face
On the mantle of liminality,

A junction between the passing and becoming,
Prismatic in her possibility
And anhiliating in her sound.

My mind is rainbow road,
Not the game on my cousin's console
But a secret fabric,
The velvety insight of some unknown thing
Becoming known.

To know is to guess
Like the sympathetic response that turns ropes into snakes.

But open the prism even slightly,
Bless my vision with crackling daggers of sanity,
And listen as the shrieks of psychosis make love to silence,
forever.

Pretty boy

Fly away, pretty boy.

A world awaits,
For you
To regret yourself early,
So lower the pangs of
Earthly starvation
For angels teeth
Don't satiate the wound,
They pamper it
In silver linings
And sugar coatings
Too pastel for anything worth grieving.

Grieve hard.
Let the triumphant underbelly
Shatter your world
With oceaning forces
Bound to the old gods.
It's a power worth heeding to.
Your numbing cream
Will fail
In the shrieking cry
Of ancient grief.

Selected Poems of Eric Fischman

In which predictions are made.

When the light touches me and not
before. When I am full in the light,
when the light hands me like a violet.
When the full color of me is fully form,
when I am structured skeletal against
the rock, when the light buries me, drowns me.
When all the trees in the light become
the light. When all the stones in the dust
become the dust. When I am flowered in
dust when the dust in the light washes
itself away. When the mountain nods,
when the last lingering cloud dusts us all
in rain. When the fog exits me, when
it enters. Only then, when the pines needling
out all colors, when the rainbow grass,
when the chipmunks asking politely,
when the flies beloved beside me

Shelter

When I was a boy I learned
not to cry. I don't know how.
I needed a wall, so I built one.
It was easy. Later I learned
that you can't tell everyone
who you are. There are shapes
to fit in public places. Two walls
with a door. They told me
I shouldn't sound so smart
if I wanted to make friends. You
have to drink, you have to have
fun. Four walls with a roof.

When I went out, I left myself
inside. I wore whatever costume
was expected of me. It was easy.
I learned to hide my anxiety, to
play parts. Bolts on the windows,
the shades drawn. What was
crying like again? I am a social
butterfly. I am a chameleon.
You will never see me bleed.
You will never feel the bruises
in my ribs. You will never even
make it to the front door.

6 Haiku for the Coming Warmth

The hill is steep,
the soil loose.
I dig my feet

It's me who watches the shadows
All they do is
touch the ground

Writing in my head,
the branch
slaps me

Trees on the hill's edge
in perpetual fall

How many ways
do I trick myself?
The cherry pit
bounces back

Poets trying so hard
not to walk through
each other's minds

I won't describe
the fluttering of the leaves
more than this

3 Non-Stop Consecutive 5-Minute Poems

Go and get yourself a goggle and a mask.
Wear these plates over your chest they aren't
kevlar but they should do. Here's a window
if it gets too hot, pull the cool glass down and
wrap it around yourself. The sound of branches
scratching the pane is the sound of blood scratching
your veins. This is entirely normal and nothing
to flail away from, babbling like the Boulder Creek,
trailing toilet paper and shoes and fireflies and dark.
The night follows like a child stumbling over
its laces. The ducks dip their webbed feet in
your generous waters how you swirl around
yourself like gravel around a rock.

Ready to go again? There are too many roads
you're welcome in all of them I'll see you at the
finish line drowning in sunset. The street is
a yellow fire, the buildings are orange fire and all
the runners spontaneously combust in red. Your feet
are fireworks and so are the cars so are the trees
the banks burning up all of Pearl Street
molten from the friction of your shoes. It's not
a race it's an afternoon, like any other day when
the earth shatters and reels calling out for Moon
her mother, heart cracking like a wheel, all of
us out from under its tongue.

Let's get back to it then the wind is still
screaming the wild eyes of the leaves blinking
ecstatically the sun won't wait for you to stand
in its heat the aspen won't stand here all day

this pen is running out of ink as fast as it
can chew. In fact nothing stands still not your
water glass not your teeth there is an army
of nerves inside you ready for shore leave.
What are you doing on the couch when every
cloud is shaped like your darkest thought
ready to blow away? Don't you know how to
whistle? Step outside, purse your lips
at the sky, and then

Cento for Ted*

It is such a good thing to be in love with you
A vast orange library of dreams, dreams
Wed to wakefulness, night which is not death
Spreads beneath the mud troubled ice
Where Snow White sleeps amongst the silent dwarfs
Each tree stands alone in stillness
Warmth comes, a slow going down of the Morning Land
The wind's wish is the tree's demand
Trillion pointed bright red-brown and green-gold
On a fragrant evening fraught with sadness
Watching the sun come up over the navy yard
The big green day today is singing to itself
Aches in rhythm to that pounding morning rain
Dear, be the tree your sleep awaits

*A cento is a poetical work wholly composed of verses or passages
borrowed from other authors. In this case, Ted Berrigan's **Sonnets**.

Thanks For Reading!

If you're interested in more check out our website

www.thewheelart.com

and follow us on Instagram

@Thewheelart_

www.ingramcontent.com/pod-product-compliance
Lightning Source LLC
Chambersburg PA
CBHW070356230526
45471CB00006B/2597